W9-CMI-516

THE TYPICAL
HUSKY

- **Forms close human-animal bond**

- **Gregarious and curious**

- **Full of playful energy**

- **Enthusiastic hunting companion**

- **Highly sociable**

- **Not easily trained**

When you see Siberian Huskies in action, it is hard to resist them. Because of their joyful demeanor, exuberance, friendliness, and striking appearance, they continue to grow in popularity. It must be emphasized, however, that this breed makes rather high demands on its owners when it comes to general maintenance and creative activities. It is not easy to satisfy these demands, particularly in areas where the dog cannot be involved in dogsledding sports.

IS A HUSKY THE RIGHT

1 Huskies live for 15 years or more, and want to spend them in close contact with their pack, their human family. Will you be able to satisfy the many breed–specific demands of this dog for that long?

2 Huskies are working dogs that need to be kept busy much of the time. Are you prepared to spend most of your free time with your Husky for more than ten years? Do you and your family love outdoor activities, even in winter and bad weather? Do you live in close proximity to running and exercise areas?

3 Huskies are extremely social. They do not like to be left alone and need to be close to humans. How much human companionship can you give to this pet?

4 Keeping a Husky can become expensive. In addition to routine expenses for food and supplies, there may be steep veterinary bills when health problems occur. Are you willing to pay in return for the pleasure of living the Husky experience?

5 Do you know a reliable person who can spend sufficient time and effort on the animal when you are traveling without it?

6 Are you aware of the fact that your Husky will shed veritable mountains of hair, twice every year?

7 Are your family members free of allergies to dog hair and dander?

8 If you intend to keep more than one Husky, be aware of the fact that they will howl from time to time. It is best to check with your neighbors whether it would be feasible to keep multiple Huskies.

DOG FOR YOU?

One or More?

This social animal does not like to be left alone. If you need to be away frequently, a companion dog, not necessarily a Husky, would go a long way to alleviate the problem of its loneliness. Huskies do very well in groups, but remember that pack living will cause them to consider other dogs as rivals. Multiple Huskies are best kept in spacious kennels. Each dog needs about 100 square feet (10 sq m), and the kennel must be absolutely escape-proof. The fence should be sunk approximately ten inches (20 cm) into cement, and should be at least six feet (1.8 m) high.

PURCHASE AND ADJUSTMENT

Huskies look very much like wolves but they are genetically no closer to their ancestor than other breeds. The resemblance is more a reflection of close adaptation to the climatic demands of this breed's country of origin.

The Ancestry of Huskies

Sled dog breeds are historically closely linked to the peoples of northern countries who depended on their dogs from the earliest days. At first, dogs were used as pack animals and for hunting; later, around 2000 BC, they began pulling sleds. This means of transportation was then—and is in many cases still today—the most important for northern peoples, including many Indian tribes. Dogs from these geographic areas were the main ancestors of today's Huskies. They were of medium size, robust, and very strong, with a dense coat, thick brushlike tail, and erect ears. The sole breeding criteria were strength, health, and a gentle disposition; the harsh environment added its own demanding traits. Over time, breed lines differentiated between dogs that were bred for speed, for ability to carry loads, and for other tasks. Eastern Siberia is the cradle of our Husky; from there they spread to Alaska, where they quickly became popular.

Since 1973 we are reminded by the annual Iditarod event of the legendary fame Huskies earned in 1925: A diphtheria epidemic broke out in Nome, Alaska, and Huskies were used in sled teams to fetch the life-saving serum from the city of Nenana, 1,000 miles (1,609 km) away.

Today Huskies are enjoying popularity in many other countries, particularly where there are dogsledding activities.

Breed Characteristics

Siberian Huskies belong to the group of working dogs that originated in Nordic countries. Their most important traits are their medium size, a well-furred body with a foxlike brush-shaped tail, and strongly erect ears. Their body type enables them to pull moderately heavy loads over long distances, their gait appears fluid and effortless. The coat consists of an outer layer of guard hairs and a dense fine, and soft undercoat. The tail is curved like a graceful sickle over the rump, never curled. It hangs down when the dog is resting and when the dog is pulling a sled. All colors are recognized, from black to pure white, as well as a variety of markings on the head. Males

Despite their strikingly beautiful appearance, the purchase of a Husky should be carefully considered.

measure 21 to 23 inches (53–60 cm) at the withers, females, 20 to 22 inches (51–56 cm). Males weigh 45 to 60 pounds (20.5–27.5 kg), females, 35 to 50 pounds (16–22.5 kg).

Character Traits of Siberian Huskies

This dog is an enthusiastic working dog, yet friendly and gentle. Highly intelligent, these animals take a keen interest in their environment, they love to play, and are quick learners. Adult Huskies may act a little more reserved, but they are never aggressive toward their human or canine companions. This breed is definitely not suitable as guard dogs; while Huskies can howl quite a tune, they are not barkers. In their ancestral home country, these dogs are left

Above all, Huskies love to play with other dogs.

much of the time to fend for themselves, which led to today's breed characteristics of independence and strong will. Despite their eagerness to learn, modern Siberian Huskies are not easy to train. In addition, one must deal with the dog's innate desire to run, to hunt, and to bond with members of a pack. This is not a dog that is meant to live a lonely life.

From an early age on, this breed requires consistent and patient training. To keep this dog happy, you must plan on extensive outdoor activities and many other diversions.

Considerations Before You Buy

The purchase of a dog requires much deliberation; no other human-animal bond is as close as that of dog and human. Siberian Huskies are exceptionally social animals that need close human or canine companionship in order to thrive. Their care and maintenance demand a great deal of time and effort, especially their need for a great deal of exercise. You should decide to get a Husky only if you have answered all the questions on page 6 with an unwavering Yes.

Male or Female?

Females are going to be in heat twice every year, beginning with a first heat at about seven to ten months. During this time, the female will try to find a male, which is going to require your keen and watchful surveillance. Males mature at the same age and they are always "ready." Males can pick up the scent of a female from miles away, and they will try to find her at all cost.

If there are more female dogs in the neighborhood, you are probably better off with a female; the same is true for males. It is generally accepted that females are just a little more easily trained but there are exceptions. Overall, Huskies get along with everyone; however, if males become irritated, they do tend to get into trouble more easily than females.

Puppy or Adult?

The first four months of life represent the most important phases in the life of the dog, literally forming the animal for the rest of its life. People who know this can influence the growth and development of their pet in a positive way by educating themselves in depth

Checklist
Before You Buy

1 Gather as much reading material about Siberian Huskies as you can possibly find.

2 Attend sporting events and shows. You can get dates and places from the AKC or from local breed clubs.

3 Consider your preferences for males or females according to your lifestyle.

4 Check whether you are permitted to keep two or more dogs on your property.

5 Secure your property by installing a fence six feet in height (1.8 m), which is cemented eight to ten inches (20 cm) into the ground.

6 Check with your veterinarian or with breed clubs where to register your new puppy to attend puppy play school and training.

7 Be ready to pick up your puppy from the breeder at eight to ten weeks.

Your Dog and the Law

If you want to own a dog you should know the answers to some legal questions.

✔ If you are renting, you must have the permission of the landlord.

✔ It is a good idea to have liability insurance for the dog.

✔ Get all necessary regulatory information from city or county offices as they relate to registration, vaccination, leash laws, etc.

about the quality of the breeder's dogs, and about the needs of growing pups.

Adult dogs have already lived through the formative phases, including good and bad experiences, so be prepared for some surprises in their behavior. Huskies are not strongly focused on one human; therefore, they usually adapt quite easily to a new environment. Choosing an adult Husky would be preferable if you know the breeder, and if you know that the dog was kept by a conscientious previous owner.

Portraits of Sled Dogs

Apart from the Siberian Husky there are three other recognized breeds of sled dogs that have evolved through selective breeding. There are also a number of nonrecognized breeds, of which the Alaskan Husky is the best known. All have a friendly disposition in common, as well as a hardy constitution, and a distinct hunting instinct. These are not dogs that are suitable for everyone.

The Alaskan Malamute

This is the largest and heaviest of the sled dog breeds at 85 pounds (39 kg) and 25 inches (63.5 cm) at the shoulders. Malamutes are quite strong and act feisty toward other dogs. These dogs need a very firm hand and consistency in training, especially when they are kept in packs. Although naturally calm and patient, this intelligent breed requires a great deal of exercise. When pulling sleds, these dogs are not fast but can pull or carry heavy loads.

The Samoyed

In its northern Russian home, this dog was used to pull sleds, to hunt, and to guard reindeer. It has great endurance and strength when pulling heavy loads. These dogs are smaller than Malamutes, 21 to 23 inches (53–58 cm), 65 pounds (30 kg); they are white or lightly yellow-tinged, with a most affectionate, gentle, and playful nature. Remember, these dogs bark. The Samoyed is strong-willed and needs a firm and sensitive hand in training. As a working dog, this breed also needs a great deal of physical activity.

The Greenland Dog

This is the roughest and most original of the Nordic breeds. In its home country, this dog is still a true Eskimo dog that is left to fend for its survival under the harshest conditions. This makes it most strong-willed, and hard to train. These dogs work hard in front of sleds. As pets, you would need to spend a lot of time on physical activities. They measure about 23 inches (60 cm) at the shoulders, weighing about 75 pounds (35 kg). (Note: This breed is not recognized by the AKC.)

The Alaskan Husky

This is the fastest of the sled dogs. The breed originated from crosses of Siberian Huskies, hunting, and hound dogs. Its background makes it easy to train, but it requires extraordinary attention to exercise. Breed selection in this case ignores appearance, paying attention solely to speed.

The Right Puppy

Siberian Huskies are really not made for our modern lifestyles that are mostly removed from nature. If you want to own a Husky because of its unusual blue eyes and elegant appearance, you will not have the long-term pleasure you might be hoping for—Huskies will soon show their discomfort when their breed-specific activities are missing.

It is very important that you educate yourself about the special needs of Siberian Huskies before you make your final decision. Dogsled races and dog shows are the best places to get valuable impressions. You can also meet other Husky owners and breeders there. Dates and locations of the events are available from the AKC and from regional clubs (see page 62). They will also refer you to currently available litters.

Siberian Huskies come in a great variety of coat colors.

PORTRAITS
OF SLED DOGS

Selective breeding has led from the original dogs of northern countries to four internationally recognized purebred sled dogs. The Alaskan Husky is not among them.

Siberian Husky, brown and white.

Greenland Dogs are true to their ancestral traits, and quite strong-willed.

Samoyeds are happy dogs, but they love to bark.

Malamutes are self-assured and very strong.

This color is acceptable for Greenland Dogs.

Speed is important for Alaskan Huskies.

Siberian Huskies are full of energy, they are enthusiastic working dogs.

Five Ways to Pick the Right Puppy

1 Get in touch with the referral system of the AKC and with your regional breed clubs (for addresses, see page 62).

2 Educate yourself by reading about the growth and development of puppies (see reading references, page 62).

3 Visit several breeders, and select the best one by considering the following criteria: cleanliness, breed-specific maintenance, and signs of close human bonding.

4 Visit the litter as often as possible and let the breeder help you select the most suitable pup.

5 Take your chosen puppy as early as possible, and throughout the formative growth period, to a puppy play school.

How to Select the Right Breeder

Plan on visiting as many breeders as you can locate in order to make valid comparisons. Consider the following points:

Today's Huskies are bred like many other dog breeds for show and sporting competitions. Show dogs compete only for their appearance. Show Huskies are, as a rule, not very hardy and tend to be more difficult to train. Sporting breed lines, on the other hand, have to show a track record of their working abilities.

Most Husky breeders are "mushers," who are involved in sledding sports, and tend to keep packs of dogs in kennels. These dogs are selected for their social and sledding abilities. Human bonding, and tolerance to traffic noise and to stairs and furniture in a home are unimportant qualities to these breeders. For a house pet, however, these would be just the traits that are necessary to keep the dog free of stress and fears.

It is important, therefore, that you select a breeder who spends quality time with the puppies, getting them used to their new environment. Remember to make sure that the litter appears healthy and playful, and that the environment is immaculate. Conscientious breeders, in turn, will make sure that the potential buyer promises a new home that fits this special breed.

The Purchase Agreement

Selecting your Husky puppy hopefully has been an enjoyable experience. Your must now formalize the agreement by putting all the terms of the deal in writing. Be precise and list not only the purchase price, but also the terms of the guarantee and what documentation will be supplied.

To guarantee that the puppy is healthy, most breeders will allow new owners a certain number of days to have the puppy examined by

This Husky howls because he is lonely.

their personal veterinarian. Get the specific terms of the deal in writing, as a verbal promise will get you nowhere legally. The agreement should specify whether a sick dog will be repalced with a healthy puppy or if the purchaser's money will be returned.

When dealing with a kennel or pet shop, the new owner of a purebred Husky should receive the puppy's American Kennel Club registration application at the time of the purchase. The application should include the names and AKC numbers of the sire and dam, information on the litter from which the puppy was whelped, and the name and address of the person to whom ownership is being transferred. The new owner must list two possible names for the puppy and complete all missing information. Processing the paperwork should take about three to four weeks, if all is in order.

Established breeders most likely will have registered the puppy's litter with the AKC shortly after birth and should have received these applications prior to the sale of any of the puppies. If

the application is not available, the new owner must get a signed bill of sale from the breeder that lists the breed, sex, and color of the puppy; its date of birth; and the registered names (with numbers) of the sire and dam. Without this information the American Kennel Club likely will be unable to register the dog.

Kennels that breed Huskies strictly for show purposes may have some additional purchase terms. The breeder may want to be involved with the future breeding of the dog or may stipulate that it will be sold only on the condition that it is shown in competition for its championship. Such concerned kennels may agree to sell a pet-quality dog only on the condition that it *not* be bred and may even withhold registration papers until proof is supplied that the dog has been neutered. In exchange

Huskies love long nature walks.

for such terms the breeder often wll offer an attractive selling price for the dog.

How to Pick the Right Puppy

For a Husky to become a good family pet, it should be gentle and eager to learn, and to bond. Do not select a pup that is fearful, shy, or aggressive. Dominant or overly sensitive dogs are not for everyone, either. Experienced, reputable breeders know parents and litters well enough to match their traits with the needs of an interested buyer.

Generally, it can be said that the dominant puppy is the one that bounces all over the place, trying to nip your clothing and fingers, while the submissive sibling licks your hands, gingerly tends its paw, and even dribbles a few drops of urine in the excitement of approaching the newcomer.

Bringing Your Puppy Home

If you plan to transport your puppy by car you should have a second person accompany you. The person who will most often be in charge of the care should be the one who attends to the dog during the drive. Bring along a collar and leash, fresh water, and a roll of paper towels.

During the trip in the car, hold the puppy on a towel or blanket on your lap or sit in the back seat and keep the pup next to you. Never place a puppy inside a box or in the trunk!

If the trip is long plan for several stops so that the pup can relieve itself and move around. Don't let it off the leash for a moment!

If you receive your Husky pup by plane or from overseas, make sure that you have prepared all necessary papers in order to avoid any unnecessary delays in its confinement.

Husky Supplies

The list of supplies on this page serves as a guide. Have everything ready when you bring the puppy home. Leash and collar should be made of leather; never use choke or spiked collars! Collar and leash should be adaptable, but a retractable leash is not recommended. Get a simple doggie bed that is washable and large enough for the growing pup. Your dog should be able to stretch out comfortably in its bed.

Your pup will also appreciate some toys and chew things.

Checklist
Supplies

1 Wide and flat collar and leash, both adjustable; leather or fabric.

2 A good-quality dog whistle; available in pet stores.

3 Bedding: high-quality pillow or mattress, sufficiently large, washable.

4 Nonslip bowls for water and food: high-quality plastic or stainless steel.

5 Rubber curry brush and combs for regular body and hair care and skin massage.

6 A few toys (from the pet store), they must be large enough so they can't be swallowed, yet small enough to be easily carried around by a pup.

7 Chew toys specifically made for puppies; a variety of materials are available.

8 Food for the first few weeks, preferably the same that was used by the breeder.

The First Days in the New Home

When you arrive at home allow the puppy to explore its new space. At this time the pup should meet only its "pack"; friends and relatives should not be introduced until later.

✔ Introduce the pup to its new sleeping quarters, its toys, and, if it is hungry, its food bowls. Do not bother the pup for attention now; it will come to sniff out each family member all on its own. Give it time. If it is sleepy do not disturb it.

✔ Plan to take several walks each day. Keep the pup on a leash. Put its bed close to yours for the night, either outside your bedroom door or right next to your bed. This will help prevent loneliness and anxiety. Once the animal is housebroken, you can choose another location for the bed. The basic rule is to not remove a Husky puppy physically from its pack.

✔ During the initial phase of adjustment, it is recommended that you continue feeding the puppy the same food that was used by the breeder. Sudden food changes can

Introduce the puppy to its sleeping area.

stress the digestive system at this critical stage. You can begin changing the food later and do it slowly over time.

Housebreaking Your Puppy

The closer you observe your Husky pup, the sooner housebreaking will be accomplished. After each meal and after it has been sleeping, take the puppy to the location where you want it to relieve itself. This should be the same place during the training period. Take it there also every time it appears

Buy all the necessary supplies before you bring your Husky home. You should have a collar and leash, food and water bowls, toys, and bedding.

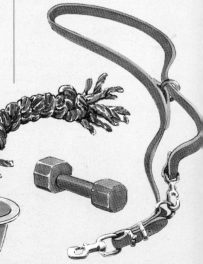

restless or walks in circles sniffing the ground. Praise the pup lavishly after it relieves itself.

Prepare its sleeping area close to yours, and try to limit its escape routes. Dogs do not like to relieve themselves in their sleeping quarters. When it gets restless, you will hear it move around and you should let it go outside. If a mishap occurs, just say "*No*," and take the pup outside. If you don't notice the mishap until later, do not comment at all, but just clean it up. Any comment or criticism at that point could not be understood by the dog and would lead to

insecurity. Make sure to disinfect the soiled area with an agent that will remove the scent so that the puppy is not inclined to do it there again.

There are some good commercial products that remove stains and odors by breaking down the enzymes in the organic matter that your dog has deposited on your carpet. You can purchase them at your pet supply store or from a catalog. Soak the stain, scrub the cleaner into the carpet with a brush, and place paper towel over the spot to absorb the liquid. Repeat, if necessary.

When you find the puppy sitting at the door, take it outside to the location where you want it to relieve itself.

Hazards

Prevent injuries inside your house and in your backyard by securing ponds, stairs, windows, and balconies with grates and screens. All backyard areas that are accessible to the puppy should be fenced in. Secure basement shafts and other holes in the ground, and remove all types of garden poisons. Remove toxic indoor plants. Check the areas to

Use turkey wire in addition to fencing.

which the pup has access for small toys, needles, and sharp small objects that could be swallowed. Remove or cover electric cables. Place carpeting on slippery surfaces to prevent

Grates keep pups from exploring holes and drains.

injuries. Do not leave a young dog for long without supervision, either indoors or outdoors. Little dogs are not much different from little children; they come up with ideas you never

thought of. Pups are also easy targets for dognappers when they are left alone in the yard.

DAILY CARE AND MAINTENANCE

The essential stages of growth and development, as well as basic character formation, take place during the first four months of a Husky's life. Both breeder and new owner must show commitment and responsibility.

The Life Stages of Dogs

Dogs undergo a distinct series of developmental phases on their way from puppyhood to old age. Each stage makes different demands on care and understanding.

The Puppy

The brain develops in specific perceptual areas during the fourteenth and sixteenth weeks. Positive and negative experiences at this time will have lifelong consequences. Lack of learning may never be made up in later life.

The newborn pup is blind, deaf, and dependent on its mother for the first two weeks of life, but essential aspects of development are underway.

Between the third and eighth weeks, the puppy learns to distinguish the members of its "pack," which includes canine and human members.

At this time it is most important for the pup to experience positive interaction and human bonding. Games of discovery are important

This Husky is waiting eagerly for his next chance at play or work.

now to expand its curious mind. The breeder carries much of the responsibility for creating a positive foundation.

From the ninth to the fourteenth week, the puppy learns to interact with other canine playmates. Its curiosity increases with further physical growth. If the puppy is going to live with other Huskies for a life of sporting activities, it may remain with its mother and litter until the end of this growth phase in order to learn social integration. If, however, the animal's future is intended as a family pet, the puppy should be in its new home by the age of ten weeks. This time is needed to form bonds with humans and other dogs (as at puppy play school events). This is also the time to get the pup used to traffic, different humans, car trips, stairs, and so on. The puppy can now learn its first commands (see Training, page 44). This is not the time to be overprotective of the young animal. It should be considered a real dog, not a baby, but that does not mean that you can overexert the pup.

Puppy play school and exercise events should now be regularly attended. Professional classes for this purpose are important for your dog, which needs to learn the difference

Growth and Development of Huskies

Stage	Indications/Observations	
Puppy		
1st and 2nd week	Eyes and ears are closed. Feeling of warmth and sense of smell are limited. Early important needs are for	body warmth and milk source. They will compete with siblings. Important developmental time.
3rd to 8th week	First stage of imprinting; sensitive stage. Physical development and mental curiosity progress. Optimal bond-	ing to humans and interaction with siblings occurs in this phase. Environmental experiences are essential now.
9th to about 14th week	Second stage of imprinting and socialization. The puppy is eager to learn and to find a place in its "pack." Increased alertness and curiosity. Now	the pup should become familiar with everything that will make up its future environment.
The Young Dog		
4th and 5th month	This phase can be considered a teenage stage. The pack instincts are being tested, imprinting has been completed. Avoid negative experi-	ences. Be consistent with previously set rules and limits.
6th to 12th month	Most impressions have been formed. Puberty and sexual maturity take place. Females go through first heat cycle; males begin marking their territory. Puberty may be accompanied by more teenage behavior. Some dogs	become shy for a short period. Continue being consistent and firm in training matters.
The Adult Husky		
End of 1st year	Physical growth is completed, while the character develops further. Full adulthood is reached by approximately the second year. Learning	experiences and new discoveries are still important factors in forming the animal for life.
The Aging Husky		
	At what age your Husky turns "old" depends largely on the way it was kept. The animal wants less activity and more lazy snoozes. A veterinary	exam is indicated every six months. Nutrition should be tailored to the overall condition of the dog.

between human and canine interactions. In guided play, the pup learns to be self-assured and how to accept discipline, while the owner learns about canine behavior. Classes should not consist of more than eight pups, and their ages should be as close as possible. Play and joy of discovery are the important experiences, not discipline. Before you attend, get references from a veterinarian or from breed clubs.

The Young Dog

The impressionable phase of the dog is completed by the third and fourth months. The fifth month might bring about a bit of a wild teenage stage, when Huskies try to compete for pack leadership and suddenly they ignore previously well-accepted commands. The second half of the first year is the puberty phase; some teen behaviors are typical also during this time. Females experience their first heat at this age; males begin to mark their territory by leaving urine trails. Consistency in training patterns is now essential, otherwise Huskies will quickly pick up bad habits.

The Adult Husky

Sexual maturity marks the end of puppyhood.

For many years to come, your Husky will be in full possession of its intelligence and strength. The main ingredients for the dog's fulfillment are curiosity, eagerness to learn and discover, and playfulness.

If you have truly committed time and effort in your Husky's first year of life, you are now its accepted pack leader and partner. If you intend to attend courses for companion dog training, now is the time to begin. Sled dogs can also be trained at this time.

They will still retain their special character traits, and will assert themselves when challenged. The type of disciplinary training that is still seen in many dog training schools is completely unsuitable for your Husky. Old-fashioned dog training will block your Husky's natural behavior, make it fearful, and may lead to aggression. These dogs need modern training that focuses on positive reinforcement, no punishment, and motivating stimuli to work.

The Aging Husky

Your dog's condition in old age depends largely on its past maintenance. Huskies age faster when they are not kept active, and when they are overfed, but there are many happy Huskies around that are eagerly pulling sleds at the age of 12; 15 and older is not uncommon for these dogs. When you notice age-related changes in your pet, be sensitive to different changing needs, such as diet (page 32) and exercise. Arthritis may have set in, its gait may appear a little stiff, and it may seek warmer quarters.

Young Huskies bond easily with other house pets.

BOONE COUNTY

Specific Maintenance for Huskies

Huskies love to run and work, and they make great companions for hiking, skiing, jogging, and biking.

Pulling sleds is still their favorite activity. Once you have experienced the exuberant happiness and excitement of Huskies before the start of a sledding event, you will understand how a Husky must suffer when it is deprived of these activities.

How Much Exercise Is Enough for a Husky?

We cannot tell you exactly how many hours you should spend outdoors with your Husky on a daily basis; however, it is certain that it needs to go outside several times a day, and during one of these occasions it must be able to really run to its heart's delight. If you do not offer enough exercise, it is likely that your pet will be unmanageable, changing your backyard and your house in a rather undesirable way. If you have a large enough yard that is fenced in, it is a good idea to invite Husky friends to visit so that the dogs can play as hard as they want to and expend the necessary energy.

Outdoor Exercise and Housing

No dogs enjoy the outdoors more than Huskies. They have flourished in some of the coldest, harshest areas on earth. The vast majority of Huskies in the United States are kept as companions in the home, but they also can adapt to being housed in a kennel building—provided there is plenty of human and canine companionship during the course of the day. Huskies are much too people-oriented to be kept strictly as kennel dogs.

Huskies should be given plenty of access to the outdoors. They thrive when allowed to

Many Huskies love to dig up the ground.

romp. They need adequate amounts of exercise to release tensions that may build up when confined to the indoors. The release they get from time outdoors keeps them more relaxed in the home and helps to thwart such negative habits as tension chewing or howling.

Huskies are very happy to spend a considerable amount of time outdoors. But no matter how hardy the breed and how impervious to the elements this breed seems, they still require proper protection from the elements. Doghouses can be constructed to provide adequate shelter against heat, cold, and dampness. It must be well insulated and large enough to

allow the dog to fully stretch out, but not too large to maintain warmth. The entrance should be just large enough to allow the dog to enter easily. A doghouse with a hinged top is easiest to clean.

The house must be placed in a shaded area during the hot months, and a sunny spot is best during cold periods. The house should be mounted on platform risers or placed on blocks to stand several inches off the ground. This keeps the house from direct contact with the soil. Do not position the doghouse directly against a fence. Although Huskies are not noted climbers, placing a house in this way gives the dog the opportunity to climb upon it and jump to freedom.

Any area that your Husky is allowed to roam in freely *must* be properly fenced, preferably to

When Huskies get a chance to play together they can use up a good deal of energy.

a height of five feet. Huskies are distracted easily by the "call of the wild" and impervious to any possible danger from passing vehicles. These traits make it extremely dangerous to allow them access to open areas. A secure run is a good solution, as it allows the dog some roaming space yet keeps it in safe confinement. Huskies also delight in digging, so the fence should be buried slightly to thwart any possible chance of tunneling under it. Most Huskies do not scheme to escape their surroundings, however. They dig for the thrill of digging and sometimes keep to their task until a hole large enough for lying down in it has been devised.

TIP

Huskies and Children

If you have children and are planning to get a Husky, here are some points to consider:

1. Children must learn that a dog requires special understanding and that the animal is not a toy; for example, they must respect the dog's need to rest, which is of particular importance for young puppies.

2. Prevent children from playing too roughly with the young dog.

3. At the time you get a Husky pup, your youngest child should be at least three or four years old. At this age children understand some of the necessary warnings, and they are not competing as intensely for "baby care" time when you need to spend time with the dog.

If Your Husky Runs Away

Make sure that your dog wears a tag with your phone number on it. As soon as you notice that the dog is missing, call the shelters in the area. Let neighbors know, post signs that describe the dog, and give your contact number. If you know where the animal took off, place a piece of clothing and put a dog treat on it; dogs have a habit of returning to the original site of their adventure. If you can't find the dog, place an ad in the local newspaper.

The Single Husky

As a rule, a single Husky should only rarely be left alone. You need to teach it at an early age to tolerate being alone for a short period at a time (see Training, page 44). Some Huskies never get used to being left alone. They may howl endlessly or try to do mischief, in which case you must be prepared to either have the dog with you wherever you go, or enlist the help of friends or dog-sitters. It may mean a lot of personal adjustments in your lifestyle. A second dog will make a big difference. If the second dog is also a Husky, you can plan on getting a sled as your next purchase.

Most mushers once started with a "family Husky." Soon after that they get the "Husky bug" and end up raising six or more offspring for sledding.

Play Time

Not only do Huskies love to play, it's also an important part of their development. While the whole body, heart, and muscles get strengthened, playing also furthers social interactive skills.

When you play with your Husky, the human-animal bond grows closer, and at the same time the dog learns to respect you as the pack leader because it learns that it is not allowed to nip you in your legs or tug on your clothing. Another way of stressing your role as the superior play partner is to not follow all of the dog's invitations to play, but, rather, you should be the one to invite it to play. It is important that you are conscious of the fact that children should not lie underneath the young dog during playtime.

If the dog loves to play by pulling such things as an old towel, make sure that, from time to time, you are the winner who gets the towel. This type of game is not suitable for small children.

Recommended games are running, ball games, and hide-and-seek. During the latter, you leave the dog in one room while the

children hide, then, with the command *"Seek,"* guide the dog in playing the game. Lavish praise is an important part of this training, so that the young dog will learn very quickly and enjoys the game.

Another favorite of Huskies is running an obstacle course, an activity that teaches agility. There are many other games to further train and entertain your dog, (see Literature, page 62).

Huskies Love Children

Huskies are exceptionally socially adaptable, bond easily, and love to play. They are not suitable as guard dogs. On the contrary, they make great companions and cuddly friends for children.

Huskies and children form close friendships as long as the children understand that dogs are not toys.

What is true for all dogs is true for the Husky: The bonding to your children will depend on the positive or negative experiences that were made between the young puppy and its first human keepers. That is the reason why it is important that you find out how your puppy was treated by the breeder, and what other type of contact the animal had before coming into your home.

VACATIONS

If you plan to take your dog along on your vacation, you need to plan ahead. Here are some tips:

1. Choose a Husky-friendly vacation goal.

2. If you plan to travel abroad, you need to have papers, vaccinations, and health certificates arranged at least two months before you leave. Airline and train arrangements may require even longer preparation.

3. Request a confirmation from the place where you are going to stay that one or more dogs are indeed accepted.

4. Prepare the right luggage for your Husky: bedding, water and food bowls, collar and leash, a whistle, and a few favorite toys. Don't forget food, a few chewable toys, and a brush. This is the time to take along an automatic leash, since the new environment may require a little more restriction during your outings.

5. For car trips, plan to take a break at least every two hours.

Vacationing with Your Husky

If you want to travel with your Husky, you need to consider the dog's special needs. If it loves car rides it will be only too pleased to go along; however, if you want to go south to sunbathe on the beach, your Husky is not the right companion.

Don't plan to leave your dog in a hotel room for extended times either—Huskies are made for active outdoor vacationing only. They love running and swimming, northern locations are preferred, and southern sites are acceptable in early spring and late fall.

If your Husky tolerates car trips well, take along plenty of water and a few snacks. Feed the last main meal several hours before you start your trip. If you have a potentially carsick pet, seek help from your veterinarian. Get advice, also, as to what you should take for canine emergencies such as digestive trouble, insect stings, or small injuries.

Some countries have quarantine laws—you can't take a dog into the country nor are you allowed to pass through it. Request customs information from consulates or from your veterinarian before you leave.

If you do not take your dog with you on your vacation, you must plan well ahead for a dog-sitter. The dog's breeder would be a good solution, but if that is not possible, get references from your veterinarian and from your local breed clubs. The ideal situation is to leave your dog in its home and have a reliable friend or family member care for it there.

Grooming Your Husky

While Huskies are low-maintenance dogs, the young Husky should get used to being groomed and handled. Get the dog familiar with such words as "Let's look at the teeth," "now the ears," and so on. This training will greatly facilitate veterinary visits and dog show presentations.

Coat Care: The Husky is a double-coated breed. This means that it has a woolly undercoat that serves as the dog's insulation against cold or heat, and a layer of longer, harsher outercoat that grows through the undercoat. Shedding will occur at least once a year in males, and twice a year (generally spring and fall) in females. High humidity or excessive heat often will make the shedding worse.

The shedding process usually will take from three to six weeks, with a new coat growing in during the next three to four months. During the active shedding period, groom the dog daily. Between shedding times, regular brushing should take care of the excess loose hairs. If you maintain a weekly grooming pattern, you should not be plagued continually by hair left behind wherever the dog has been, as is common with some other breeds.

The main aim of grooming is to remove dead hairs that are clinging to the coat. In the process, you are also cleaning the skin and the shafts of the living hair. The main tools for grooming the Husky are a wide-toothed comb and a bristle brush. The tips of the comb's teeth must always be rounded, and the bristles of the brush must be long enough to reach through the coat to the skin. The Husky's coat is not to be cut or trimmed—ever. Very minor tidying of stray hairs may occur around such areas as the feet in show dogs, but any shaping or stripping of the Husky's coat is unwarranted.

The comb should be used to run through the coat to break up any mats or snags and to remove the dead hairs. Knots should be worked out a little at a time, using the comb and the

This team is looking forward to their trip with happy anticipation.

fingers to gently tease the hairs apart. It especially is important to comb through the undercoat during shedding. A fine-toothed comb is handy for the areas under the chin and tail and between the ears. Use the brush once the combing is complete to finish off the coat. Brush the coat forward, over the head and shoulders, before combing it back. Brush the rear areas in the direction of the lay of the coat. Extra attention should be given to the hindquarters, as guard hairs in this area often accumulate into mats.

Paws and Nails: Check the footpads regularly, especially if your Husky is in training. Treat dry and broken pads with Vaseline. Get booties for your dog at a pet store if it needs to run on hard ice or other rough terrain.

Nails grow long if the dog does not run much on hard surfaces. Purchase a proper nail clipper. Be careful not to cut the blood vessel in the nail. If you are inexperienced let a veterinarian show you how. If you notice that the elbows are starting to scab or get dry, rub them regularly with Vaseline.

Eyes and Ears: The eyes and ears of Huskies have maintained their natural shapes and are practically trouble-free. If you see the need to clean the ears, use a little baby oil on a soft

cloth and wipe only the outer part of the ear canal. To wipe the corners of the eyes, use a moist, very soft cotton cloth.

Teeth: Well-fed Huskies rarely have teeth problems Daily, give your dog a hard dog biscuit, a large chew bone, or any such chewable item. When the adult teeth break through, check your puppy's mouth to make sure the milk teeth are falling out.

Should You Bathe Your Husky? Huskies love water but you should not bathe your Husky with detergents or other additives. When a bath is absolutely necessary, use only special dog shampoo. Have the animal stand on a nonslip surface in the tub or shower. Rinsing out all of the shampoo from the Husky's thick coat is very important. Towel the coat as thoroughly as possible and prevent drafts and cold air from blowing on the dog.

Proper Nutrition

A nutritious diet is most important for the general well-being of your Husky. A look at the diet of wolves gives good insight: Despite 10,000 years of evolution from wolf to pet, the digestive tract has changed very little. The original wolf diet is, therefore, still a valuable comparison. Wolves and dogs are carnivores. Food from prey animals ranges from a small mouse to elk. Wolves also eat fruit. Prey animals are almost completely consumed, including muscle meats and all internal organs, bones, and so on.

Our dogs, on the other hand, are totally dependent on what we humans feed them. There are as many right ways to feed your dog as there are ways to make mistakes.

Types of Food

Today it is easy to feed your dog well because of the great variety of commercially available foods. There are complete foods available, and many types of supplements.

Supplemental foods may consist of meats, vegetables, or grains. One component must complement the others.

Complete foods contain all nutrients in the correct proportions. Choose products without colors and preservatives, which may cause allergies.

Dry, kibbled food is manufactured in a variety of nutrient compositions depending on the dog's age and needs, whether it is for a puppy, for maintenance, for high performance, or for such special dietary needs as controlling weight or avoiding food allergies. Another advantage of kibbled food is that it's easy to take along when traveling.

Home-Cooked Meals

This choice is quite time-consuming but it gives you the advantage of preparing meals specifically for your pet. It is most important to make sure that all nutrients are properly balanced, including minerals and vitamins.

Raw meats offer the highest-quality protein content. It is usually available in frozen bulk form in specialty stores. It is a myth that dogs become aggressive when they eat raw meats. If you are not sure of the quality of the meat source, you should cook it for at least 30 minutes.

A well-balanced diet keeps your Husky fit and full of energy.

Vitamins, Minerals, and Trace Minerals

If you feed your dog commercial food it will get everything it needs. If, however you prepare home-cooked meals, it is critical not to add too much or too little of the supplements.

If you want to take charge of your dog's nutrition, you should get as much information as you can, from manufacturers of dog food and from reading specialty books on this subject.

Husky Particulars

Too many carbohydrates may lead to excess gas production because an imbalance between stomach acid and intestinal digestive processes can develop.

Most Important: Water

Dogs can survive for only a few days without water, while they can survive without food for several weeks. An average Husky of about 50 pounds (22 kg) requires approximately 3.5 pints (1.5 L) of water daily. The animal needs double that amount or more if such demands as races, heat, or other stress are made on its body. If the main food consists of dry kibble, the need for fresh water is even more critical.

Water should be offered fresh daily, and any remaining from the previous day should be discarded.

HOW-TO: FEEDING

How Much Food?

If you use commercial foods, follow the instructions on the package or box. Some of these guidelines are on the generous side and, since dogs have individual patterns of metabolism, you will need to watch your pet's body outline. The waist should be clearly visible, and you should feel the ribs but not see them. The same is true for puppies. Being overweight is unhealthy for your pet!

These Foods Should Be Off-limits for Your Husky:

✔ Uncooked pork and poultry

✔ Poultry bones (other bones only rarely)

✔ Sweets

✔ Spicy dinner scraps

✔ Legumes (peas, beans)

Diet Plan for Home-Cooked Meals (Daily Rations)

Puppies from 8 weeks (approx. 13 lbs. [6 kg])	Young Dogs, starting at fourth month (approx. 25 lbs. [10–12 kg])	Young Dogs from sixth month (approx. 35–40 lbs. [15–16 kg])
14 ounces (400 g) beef heart 5 ounces (140 g) supplemental food ½ ounce (15 g) mineral supplements or 7 ounces (210 g) high-quality puppy kibbles 3½ ounces (100 g) natural beef tripe	14 ounces (400 g) beef heart 6 ounces (170 g) supplemental food 0.7 ounce (20 g) mineral supplements or 7½ ounces (220 g) high-quality puppy kibbles 5 ounces (150 g) unprocessed beef tripe	21 ounces (600 g) beef heart 7 ounces (200 g) supplemental food 1 ounce (30 g) mineral supplements ½ ounce (15 g) cornflower oil or 10½ ounces (300 g) high quality junior dog food (dry) 8½ ounces (250 g) unprocessed beef tripe
Dogs from 10 months	Adult dogs (Maintenance Diet)	High-Performance Diet (for runners and sled dogs)
7 ounces (200 g) beef head meats 12 ounces (330 g) beef heart 9 ounces (250 g) supplemental food 1 ounce (35 g) vitamin/mineral mix	7 ounces (200 g) beef heart 7 ounces (200 g) unprocessed beef tripe 5 ounces (150 g) supplemental food	9 ounces (250 g) beef head meats 19 ounces (540 g) high-quality dry kibbles (35 % protein, 25% fat) ⅓ ounce (10 g) vitamin/mineral supplements

Dietary Rules

1 Establish a routine by feeding your dog at the same time every day.

2 The food should be at room temperature, never hot or straight from the refrigerator.

3 The meal should not be of a consistency that is thinner than oatmeal.

4 If you feed commercial diets, there are no additional meats or supplements necessary. Supplements are only for prepared diets described on page 34.

5 You can make the diet more interesting by occasionally adding eggs, yogurt, cottage cheese, fruit, or cooked vegetables.

6 Never save leftover foods. Discard them.

7 Make sure that cool, clean water is available for your dog at all times.

Make sure the puppy does not get too much food; overfeeding leads to health problems.

From the third to the sixth month, your puppy should have four meals a day. You may still feed some milk. Follow with three meals until the ninth month; reduce to two meals until the pup is one year old. From then on, one basic feeding is enough; however, many dogs do better when the food is divided into two meals.

Puppies need several daily meals.

Breeding

The experience of watching a litter of puppies from birth is truly wonderful, but remember, that it is also a time full of hard work, requiring special knowledge.

Important Considerations

Space is a major factor for raising a litter of Huskies—An apartment in a high-rise building is not a suitable place. You will need a special room indoors, as well as a yard for outdoor activities. Ask yourself why you want to breed. Female dogs do not need to have a litter to be healthy. If you want to breed because you want one additional pup, remember that a litter may consist of ten pups.

Once you have made up your mind that you want to breed, you need to find the right female, and if you want your male as stud Husky, he must conform to the standards. Siberian Huskies are getting more popular all the time. This has the disadvantage of encouraging indiscriminate breeding for profit, and the result is a decline in general breed quality.

To maintain the high quality of Huskies, it is essential that only recognized quality breed stock be used. Get in touch with your regional sled dog association in order to see that your dog receives the necessary ratings. High quality includes positive character traits as well as appearance and health. Before you plan to breed your dog, it is essential that you inform yourself on the requirements for responsible propagation of Huskies.

In addition, you need to look at your own pet with a critical eye: A dog intended for breeding should be strong and vital in its own newborn phase, that is, it must be able to survive without human assistance. This ensures that hereditary weaknesses are reduced. If your own dog does not fulfill all of the highest breed standards, accept this knowledge and resist the temptation to breed this animal or the entire breed will eventually suffer. How to breed and where to get breed contacts can be found through the addresses given on page 62.

Basic Biology

The heat cycle: Bitches experience heat cycles every six months. The cycle begins with a mucoid-blood-tinged discharge. The animal is ready to mate between the tenth and fifteenth day, at which time the discharge is clear and pink. At this stage the female is introduced to the male stud.

If you do not intend to breed and you have an intact female, you must be very watchful during her heat because she will try anything to get out and find a mating partner. During this time, she also exhibits other behavioral changes, such as being more needy for touch and being less obedient.

Mating: For the mating act, the female is taken to the male. They should be allowed to behave naturally and should not be forced in any way. If mating does not take place, it may be the wrong day or the dogs may not be well

Breeding Huskies is a highly responsible undertaking.

matched. The dogs are "tied" during mating, and they cannot separate. This stage may last from minutes to hours. Never try to separate the dogs!

Pregnancy and birth: Successful mating is followed by pregnancy. Now, the diet should contain more protein, fat, and vitamins, and the bitch should not be allowed to overexert herself.

Meticulous planning and selection are essential in order to maintain the breed characteristics.

About 63 days later, the puppies will be born. The bitch knows instinctively how to proceed during the birthing event, but you should inform your veterinarian prior to the date in case you need emergency assistance.

TRAINING AND COMMUNICATION

The Siberian Husky has not yet lost its breed characteristics because of overbreeding as other dogs have; it is still a true working breed. This results in a demanding training and activity schedule for you and your new companion.

Behavior Traits

The Siberian Husky is still a fundamentally natural dog. It is not altered by inbreeding and has, therefore, retained a natural canine method of communication. The erect standing ears can move to various positions, and the face has many expressions. The expressive face is further enhanced by a typically light-colored area around the mouth, that resembles that of wolves. Another important factor in communication is the Husky's naturally carried tail, not to mention its magnificent fur that can be made to stand out to impressive dimensions. Add to this the canine communication systems of touch, scent messages, and voice. Communication is usually not made up of only one signal but rather of a combination of sounds, expressions, and types of behavior. Some of the behavior is instinctive, while other types must be learned from canine or human companions.

or the price of a treat, your Husky may oblige ith a trick.

Body Language

This is the major part of communication.

Play behavior: By lowering its torso and head, the Husky invites you to play. This is also expressed by pushing its nose at you, by jumping up playfully, and by circling.

Assertive behavior: When your Husky tries to impress another dog, it walks erect and stiffly, and its hair on the back and neck stand up, making it look larger. Its ears are pointed forward, and its neck and tail are carried upright. The same behavior is expressed by scratching following marking or defecating.

Threatening Behavior: There are threats of aggression and of defense. Threats of aggression progress from trying to impress by baring the teeth, extending the ears outward, and staring straight at the opponent. A lesser-ranking dog threatens defensively by pulling the corners of the mouth back, baring the back teeth, pulling the tail under, and laying the ears flat.

Submission: Dogs signal their submission, as in ending an altercation with another dog, by lying on their back with their tail between their legs. The ears are held flat against the head, the mouth is closed with the corners of

the mouth pulled back. This is called passive submission.

This type of submission tells the higher-ranking dog—or human—that the animal wants to please the higher partner. To show this intention it licks the other's mouth, wags its tail, and lowers itself to appear small. In extreme submission, it dribbles urine. Do not interpret this as lack of cleanliness; under no circumstances punish the dog.

Vocal Communication

Barking and howling: Huskies rarely bark, usually only when they are very excited. Mostly they howl, especially when they are kept in groups. This enhances pack bonding.

Young Huskies are always active. These two are out scouting.

A lonely Husky howls from sadness and a sense of loss.

Growling: Growling signals a warning, mostly in conjunction with threat behavior. Huskies growl also when they notice something suspicious, or when they feel the need to defend their food from other dogs.

Whining and wailing: Whining sounds may be an expression of submission toward a higher-ranking dog, or they may show that the dog is excited about something. A sudden high-pitched yelp is usually a sign of pain.

The World of Scents

The nose is the dog's best developed sense. We may never fully know the extent to which dogs gather information by picking up scents but we do know that dogs leave each other scent messages that are read like a canine newspaper.

Sniffing: Dogs sniff other dogs' excreta to find out who was there. To find out more about another dog, they sniff each other's anal area, as well as the face.

Scent marking: Males mark their territory with urine in order to indicate "I was here." Some scent marks are covered by fresh urine, while others are examined, accompanied by scratching and growling. Females scent mark particularly while they are in heat in order to attract as many males as possible.

Social Behavior

Huskies are socially very well-balanced, nonaggressive, and playful. They adapt easily to other house pets and other dogs. Their pack—whether canine or human—is the center of their lives. This is definitely not a one-man dog breed, nor is the Husky suited as a guard dog; Huskies are animals that love just about any visitor.

Devoted Hunters

Huskies have a very strong hunting instinct. The only way to control this trait is by consistent firm training beginning at an early age (page 46).

While your Husky is still very young, it has to be taught that digging for mice and chasing after other animals is not acceptable. When you take a grown Husky for a walk, it is important to be prepared for signs of instinctual hunting behavior. The time to react is the minute you observe your dog sniffing on the ground excitedly, or staring fixedly at "something potentially huntable" in the distance. If you miss that minute, the dog will be off and running, and you must whistle or sternly call it back. Should you notice a cat, a wild animal, or another creature before your dog notices it, immediately place the dog on a short leash. Avoid, at all cost, ever having your Husky catch a "prey," even if it is only a bird. The success would feel so gratifying to the dog that the urge to catch more prey would increase. Keep your Husky strictly on a leash in wilderness areas or if you practice obedience training in the presence of such animals as cats or chickens. In order to offer your hunter alternative activities, create such games as hide-and-seek, and arrange interesting outings. Motivational treats and favorite toys work well to entice the dog to balance across a fallen tree trunk, to course through trails of rough terrain, and to crawl under simple home-built structures. Be creative, but use caution to avoid injuries.

INTERPRETING
BEHAVIOR

This is the body language of Huskies. They communicate this way with each other and with their humans.

 This is my Husky's behavior.

 What is my Husky saying?

 This is the right way to respond!

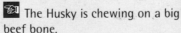

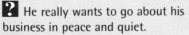

 The Husky howls.

 A single Husky howls because of loneliness.

 Increase close contact with your pet.

 Two young dogs are digging.

 It is obvious that they found something very interesting.

 Check whether there is anything there that could hurt them.

 The Husky is chewing on a big beef bone.

 He really wants to go about his business in peace and quiet.

 Okay, but he must tolerate his human pack leader removing his bone without fighting over it.

 The Husky exhibits mild threatening behavior.

 He is ready to attack his opponent.

 Do not slow your step; walk ahead briskly.

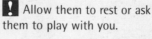 A puppy displays this lowered head and chest posture.

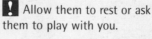 He wants his friend to play with him.

! Let them play! Playing is an important part of development.

The bitch 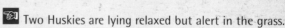 bites her pup oss the muzzle.

? This is an educational gesture.

! Allow the itch to follow her instinct.

A Husky focuses on a specific point.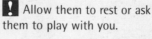

Maybe he saw a duck. ?

Call him back in time. !

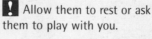 Two Huskies are lying relaxed but alert in the grass.

? They are inactive but ready for anything.

! Allow them to rest or ask them to play with you.

The Husky lies on his back in a very 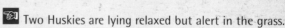 relaxed fashion.

This is a happy Husky that wants to ? be petted.

Pet and scratch his belly generously. !

Training Rules

Follow these guidelines so that your Husky can understand you, and in order to give it a sense of self-assurance and trust.

✔ Basic training should be executed by only one person, the human pack leader. The rest of the family must agree on what the dog may and may not do.

✔ Spend about five minutes three times every day while the pup is young. Create variety and always finish with an exercise that the puppy has already learned.

✔ Use your voice and body language to underline commands.

✔ Figure out what will attract your puppy's attention more than anything else in order to have its full attention. Treats, sounds, and praise words are important here.

✔ Never forget to release a previously given command. Once your Husky has understood the meaning of your command, it should follow the command on the first try. If it tries to ignore your command, use a corrective grip at the scruff of the neck.

✔ Make sure each training exercise is identical when you repeat it. Dogs cannot understand diversity in this respect, and it would lead to a feeling of insecurity.

✔ Reward each correct response to a command with praise. To be effective, the reward must immediately follow the behavior.

Proper Training

Some people say that Huskies can't be trained and you can't let them run free. If you listen to this you condemn yourself and your dog to a life on a leash, then, on the first occasion that it gets a moment of freedom, it is sure to be off and running.

While there are a number of Huskies that are quite independent, there are just as many that learn obedience eagerly, that can be trusted to run free, and that come when they are called. When you ask the owner of these dogs, you are usually told that training was consistent and serious when the Husky was a young pup. In other words, your training efforts will be richly rewarded.

It is true that Husky independence, hunting instinct, and the urge to run free are traits that make training it a little harder than some other breeds, but that only means that training must be correctly planned and consistently performed from day one. Above all, remember: Consistency, patience, and trust are the essential factors. Your puppy must learn what you want the adult Husky to know.

How to Praise Your Dog

Praise is the most important part of Husky training. As soon as the dog has accomplished a desired behavior, praise must follow in the form of stroking, a treat, and verbal approval.

You should reward each correctly executed command with the same desirable treat or praise.

Proper Discipline

Discipline is part of every dog's life. If a "bad deed" has been committed, there is only one time to correct the behavior, and that is immediately. The sound of your voice is critical when you pronounce a stern "*No.*" This may be accompanied by a firm grip reaching from the top over the muzzle. Another effective method is to grasp the dog's scruff of the neck firmly, and push it downward, holding the grip for a minute or two. Keep words and sounds consistent. If the deed is very grave, you need to act with lightning speed, grabbing the pup and turning it on its back. Hold it there until it lies still on its own accord. Be careful not to hurt the pup.

Indirect Training

Indirect training methods teach the dog its ranking order within the family without verbal instructions or manual intervention. From the first day on, all elevated surfaces such as sofas, beds, and armchairs must be off-limits.

If the dog gets its food at about the time the family eats, members of the family should finish their meal first, without giving the dog any scraps from the table.

When the animal lies in your way, do not step over it, but make it move to let you pass.

All of these directions establish you as the dominant pack leader, which is most important with such an independent breed as the Husky.

The Human–Animal Bond

Close bonding is essential for a life of harmony between you and your Husky; breed-specific training is a necessary part. This includes playing together, making new discoveries, and performing training exercises. Your Husky needs physical as well as mental stimulation.

During your daily walks you should let your puppy run free as often as possible. If you call or attract its attention with sounds and it does not come, turn and walk in the opposite direction, or hide. The pup will instinctively feel lost, and try to reestablish contact with its "pack." As soon as it comes to you, give it lavish praise. This will teach it not to lose contact.

When your puppy is tired, lie down with it on the floor. This gesture imitates a type of contact-resting that the pup has experienced with its mother and siblings.

However, discourage rough-housing on the floor, or the pup will think of you not as the pack leader, but as a littermate with the same ranking in the pack order. If your Husky thinks of you as an equal, you will not be able to train it effectively.

Resting together after a good game enhances bonding.

On these pages you will learn how to teach your Husky the basic obedience commands: sit, come, down, heel, and stay. Start training the pup after a period of adjustment and when the animal knows its name. Proceed the same way if you have adopted an adult dog. Remember, follow each correct behavior with a reward.

Sit

Hold a treat over the head of the puppy and wait until it sits to look up. Repeat the command *"Sit"* several times and praise the dog generously each time it sits. Just before it gets up, say *"Go," "Run,"* or something similar, which signals that the exercise is over. Later, you can teach that the empty hand, when held up, means to remain sitting. If sitting does not take place naturally, push gently on the little behind until the pup gets the idea.

This is the right position for "Down." Reward the pup with long strokes along its back.

Down

Hold a treat in front of the sitting puppy, and slowly guide it downward, then slightly forward. Once the dog is in the right position, give the command, *"Down"* several times and give it the treat and a rewarding pat. Before it has a chance to get up, let it sit again prior to ending the exercise (see above). Later, it will learn that the downwardly held hand, even without a treat, means to stay in the *down* position. If a *down* command is not followed, assist the instruction by gentle pressure on the upper back.

Heel

First you must decide on which side you want your Husky to heel. If it is the left side, put it on a leash and hold the leash *loosely* in the right hand. Hold a treat in your left hand and let the hand hang downward. Now, say the command, *"Heel"* and start walking briskly. Meanwhile, your puppydog is nibbling on the treat, happily walking along. As soon as a distraction occurs, get its focus and attention back to your hand. Proceed like this only a few yards each time, and finish each exercise with the *sit* command. Once the dog has understood the meaning but still gets distracted, offer

The simplest of all commands is "Sit."

one occupy the animal in another room. When you are ready, whistle and call the dog's name at the same time. As soon as the dog comes running, it gets the "exclusive" treat, verbal praise, and then its regular meal. Practice this at least three times each day for a few days, then begin practicing outside and between meals, and finally practice in other locations.

If the puppy comes when called, reward it with a treat and lavish praise.

Come

This is, without a doubt, the most important command. A dog whistle is more effective than your voice for this command because it carries over longer distances. At first this exercise is practiced only indoors, and only in conjunction with a specific treat. While you prepare the dog's meal, have some- more treats and a tug on the leash to get its attention.

Staying Alone

Wait with this lesson until the pup is at least four months old. At first, leave the animal alone for only a few minutes, and only during its natural resting period. Extend the time very slowly. Leave the dog something to nibble on while it is left alone.

Stay

Once the dog knows *sit* and *down*, begin to distance yourself, a short distance at a time, holding the leash very loosely and saying *"Stay"* in a calm voice. After a short time, give a release word (such as "O.K."), then praise the dog. Gradually increase the time you want the dog to stay, and gradually move farther away from it, always using the words *"Stay"* and the same release word each time. If the dog moves out of position, calmly and firmly put it back in place, repeating, *"Stay."*

This Husky has already learned to stay.

Breed-specific activities, particularly pulling, enhance the well-being of your Husky. The following is a list of options.

Pulling a Cart or Sled—for one or two dogs

There are a variety of carts and sleds available to please any hobby musher's heart, whether training on snow or on the road (see Addresses, page 62). Lightweight and folding models are also available. The sacco cart, for example, weighs 70 pounds (32 kg) and can be used with or without snow. Prices range from $300 to $2,000. Many other accessories are available for beginners and experienced dog owners.

Tow-training without snow.

Training to Pull

To start out, train your Husky on soft surfaces such as forest trails, or sand. Go slowly and be careful not to strain the animal. During the summer months you should train only in temperatures below 60°F (15.6°C), early mornings, and in the shade only. Your local club will assist you with useful advice.

Bicycle Training for One or Two Dogs

For this type of training you need a mountain bike or a roller bike. The belt and towline are fixed either below the handlebars or around your waist. For both models there is a quick release mechanism to prevent accidents. The dog wears a special tow harness, and the speed must keep the rope taut.

The Pulk

This is a small one-person sled to be pulled by one to three dogs. The sled requires a special tow harness that is connected to the musher with a rope and belt. The musher runs on cross-country skis behind the sled. During the snow-free season the sled is replaced by a tiny cart, and the musher jogs behind the team.

Getting Used to Pulling

Huskies can get acquainted with their harness at about seven months. The harness must be fitted to the size of the young dog. While it

Jogging together keeps dog and master fit.

was trained to walk at your heel on a loose leash, now the Husky has to learn to pull as soon as it is in a harness. It will understand the difference very quickly. Attach the leash between your belt and the dog's harness, and

Other Activities

Hiking: Hiking trips with your Husky are wonderful exercise for the entire family. Special backpacks, in which the provisions are carried, are available for your dog. Huskies can carry up to one-third of their body weight. The packs must be fitted for the size of your dog, and the animal must be

trained to carry them. *Agility and coursing sports:* In both of these sporting activities the dog is taught speed and agility by run-

Huskies carry camping provisions in special backpacks.

ning a course of such obstacles as hurdles and tunnels and. running a course of varying terrain. Huskies are highly suited for these sporting activities. To participate in some of these strenuous activities, the owner must also be physically quite fit. If you have any doubts, see your doctor for a checkup.

Practice until the dog has learned to connect its decision with your command.

Bicycle Outings

Biking without pull action is also a great Husky activity. The command *"Bike"* will let the dog know that it has to run on a loosely held leash on the right side of your bike. The leash is attached at the bike with the help of a specific lock/release mechanism.

encourage the dog to pull by saying *"Go."* Never walk ahead or parallel to the dog. Begin with very short distances, and always remember to praise the animal. When you are finished, clearly give the command *"Whoa,"* which means *"Stop."* When the dog is a year old, you can let it pull a child's sled or a car tire. Always start with short distances and low weight, and increase either very gradually.

Left and right: The international commands are *"Gee"* for right, and *"Haw"* for left.

They are distinctly different-sounding words. Of course, you may say *"Right"* and *"Left"* for home use. To teach these commands, let your dog pull you straight ahead and aim in a direction where the animal must make a turn. As soon as it aims at one of the directions, give the command you have chosen. Remember to praise immediately.

Good work is rewarded with a tasty snack to chew on.

Sled Team Sports

A book on Huskies would not be complete without mentioning sled team sports. Sled team sports are by no means a modern invention. The original Siberian people who bred this dog, as well as the Inuit Indians later, raced their sled teams to and from their places of work and hunting.

Today's style of sled team sports was born in Alaska toward the end of the last century. Races began during the Gold Rush days in the areas of Fairbanks and the Klondike. The object, then, was speed. Small private events soon developed into large international competitions that today take place annually. Still famous today are the North American Championship Sled Dog Races, which cover a 70-mile (113-km) stretch in three days, and the Fur Rendezvous Sled Dog Race in Anchorage, which also lasts three days. Then there is the Yukon Quest, as well as the Beringia on Kamchatka Island near the Bering Sea. The most famous and most grueling is the Iditarod Trail Race, usually referred to as "The Race." It spans a distance of 1,000 miles (1,600 km) between Anchorage and Nome (see page 9).

Dog sledding and racing are enjoying ever-increasing popularity, both in the United States and Europe. The International Sled Dog Racing Association (see ISDRA, page 62) sanctions races and assures their fairness and safety. Many dog breeds are allowed to participate in sled dog racing competitions.

Race Classes

The various race classes are grouped by the number of dogs per team, and by the distance and type of trails. Even with a single dog one can participate in races that cover a distance of six to eight miles (8–12 km). The highest class allows more than eight dogs, and the distance extends over 15 miles (20 km) or more. Over time many types of dog teams have been established; so has the Scandinavian style of the "pulk-class" evolved to have the mushers ski next to their dogsled team. This style was developed for the type of narrow, curving, and forested trails found in Scandinavia. In the United States, the majority of races are run by teams of dogs that run in pairs. In races where paired dog teams pull the sled, a single lead dog usually runs at the head. The musher stands on the runners of the sled.

Racing

If you plan on sledding as a sport, be prepared to invest all of your spare time and a considerable amount of money. During the winter months it is easy to find competitive races every weekend, but training continues in summer with the use of specifically built training carts. Huskies are truly happy when they are

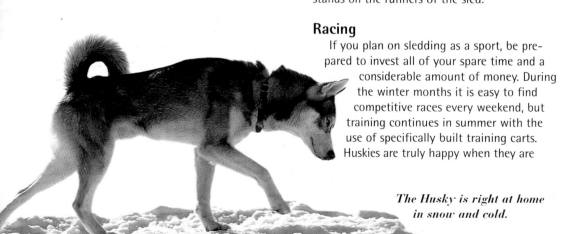

The Husky is right at home in snow and cold.

competing, and mushers often get hooked on
the sport as well. Once you have seen them run,
or if you have a chance to accompany a musher,
you can understand the exaltation. There are
clubs that can arrange for your Husky to be "on
loan" to mushers for sled race training.

If you have already caught the "Husky bug,"
you can contact a number of clubs (see page
62) that specialize in getting interested part-
ners together to form teams. Building a racing

*Confidence and excitement explode when
Huskies run in the snow.*

team and training a competitive group of dogs
take careful planning both for the mushers and
for the animals. Racing is a physically demanding sport and extensive equipment is required.
Unfortunately, this subject is too involved for
this book.

HEALTH CARE

Huskies have been carefully bred according to standards of health and performance. While this has led to an absence of breed specific diseases, your Husky may get sick one day; you should be able to provide appropriate preventive care.

Routine Maintenance

After a few days of adjustment in your home, your puppy should be taken for a general veterinary checkup. This gives the young dog a chance to experience a positive clinic visit without stress or pain.

Vaccination Plan

Vaccinations protect the animal from potentially fatal diseases. Regular boosters are needed throughout its life. The breeder will provide you with the vaccination record in which you continue to enter future records.

The first immunizations are received at about eight weeks. They include distemper-hepatitis, parvovirus, parainfluenza, and leptospirosis vaccine, followed by a booster at twelve weeks and again at three to four months, when rabies vaccine is added.

Yearly boosters of all immunizations begin at one year. Complete vaccination records are required for participation in shows and for traveling abroad.

uskies are robust dogs that are rarely ill.

Make sure that the breeder provides you with complete records of timely vaccinations.

Worm Treatments

In addition to vaccinations, dogs need to be treated for worms. Parasites weaken the animal and some types of worms can be transmitted to humans. Children are particularly susceptible.

Most puppies are infested with roundworms before they are born. They should be treated by the time they are six weeks old.

The second worm treatment should precede the first immunization; this should be repeated just before the second vaccination date. The subsequent worming should be done between six and nine months, then once or twice yearly.

If you have small children in the house, it may be a good idea to have the dog checked more frequently for evidence of worms. In order to prevent infestation with a variety of worms such as hookworm, whipworm, or tapeworm, some veterinarians treat dogs prophylactically. If you prefer, you may choose to have the dog's stool checked and treat your pet only if it is necessary. Prior to annual vaccinations, however, your dog should be treated

for worms. Additional treatment is advised if your dog catches mice and if the dog has fleas; both are sources for tapeworm infestation.

A bath in open nature can't harm your Husky, on the contrary, it loves to swim.

Skin and Hair

External parasites include fleas, lice, mites, and ticks. Ticks should be removed with a tick tweezer, or by gently turning and pulling with your fingertips. Try not to break off the head of the tick. Increased itching and eczema are signs of ectoparasites. Lice, fleas, and ticks can be easily recognized; mites leave reddish-brown deposits on the skin.

All ectoparasites, except ticks, should be treated by a veterinarian. The dog may need special baths or dips. Its living quarters must also be treated.

Skin problems in the form of eczema, hair loss, or blisters may be caused by fungi or mange, or by hormonal disorders or allergies. Zinc deficiency has been observed to cause facial eczema in Huskies.

These symptoms indicate the need for veterinary treatment. Always pay attention to cleanliness while you are taking care of your dog; some fungal infections can be transmitted to humans.

The Digestive System

Diarrhea and vomiting: If your dog has a bout of diarrhea without symptoms of general illness, place it on a one-day fast with thin black tea as liquid intake. On the following day, add cooked rice. Severe diarrhea that contains mucus or blood, or is accompanied by fever, must be treated by a veterinarian. The same is true for repeated vomiting, especially if the dog appears generally ill, has a fever, or is constipated. Constipation alone may be a sign of general disease, and the dog should be seen by a veterinarian.

Gastric torsion: This condition is indicated when the dog appears to be choking, there is increased salivation, the animal tries to vomit unsuccessfully, and the belly appears distended right after a meal. The dog is in extreme danger, and must be rushed to a veterinarian immediately. To prevent this condition, do not feed your dog large quantities at one meal, and don't let it play hard for about an hour after it has eaten.

Muscles and Bones

If you notice that your dog has a slight limp, examine the leg and foot for thorns or other small objects. If no injury is visible, give the dog a rest for a few days. Should the dog not show any improvement, you should have the animal examined by a veterinarian. If you notice that the dog has trouble getting up, has a severe limp as well as pain, swollen limbs, or fever, you should consult a veterinarian as soon as possible.

Hip dysplasia: This is a malformation of the pelvic and leg bones that causes more or fewer problems depending on the severity of the condition. It is rare in Huskies, but the dog should be diagnosed properly at about one year. Hip dysplasia is classified according to the degree of malformation.

The Sensory Organs

Huskies depend on the reliability of their senses, and you need to check them carefully.

Checklist
Performing a
Health Checkup

Follow this guide regularly to keep your Husky healthy:

1 Is its fur shiny and dense, and the skin without irritation, scabs, or sores?

2 Are the eyes, ears, and nose normal without signs of redness, discharge, or odor?

3 Are food and water intake normal? Do you notice excessive drinking or weight loss despite normal food intake?

4 Is the dog alert and curious and not overly tired, even after hard play?

5 Is its mobility unrestricted or are there noticeable problems after running or when it tries to stand?

6 Is the digestion working normally: Is the stool well formed? Are bowel movements regular?

Nose: Sniffles, sneezing, or a nasal discharge indicate a disorder of some type. The nares may be inflamed and form pus or crusts. A virus may be the culprit. Consult a veterinarian.

Eyes: Eye problems are characterized by red or swollen conjunctivas, by tearing, discharge, and by a prolapsed third eyelid. Also, small particles may lodge in the eye and lead to a milky-appearing corneal inflammation. Eye disorders must be treated by a veterinarian.

Ears: If your dog holds its head to one side, shakes its head repeatedly, or scratches its ears, it is probably having some type of ear trouble. A foul smell or dark-colored deposits often accompany such conditions.

There are a variety of causes, and you should consult a veterinarian as soon as you notice the symptoms.

Other Reasons to Consult a Veterinarian

You should consult a veterinarian any time you notice a distinct change in the appearance or behavior of your Husky. An older dog would benefit from a veterinary exam every six months, whether or not you notice changes. Have the following answers ready:

After a bath this high tree looks just right to relax on and dry off.

✔ Does the animal have a fever?
✔ What are your observations?
✔ How do urine and stool appear? Has the dog vomited?
✔ When was the dog last vaccinated and treated for worms?
✔ Has the dog had previous diseases?
✔ What is the normal diet pattern?
✔ How and where is the dog kept?

How to Recognize Health Problems

Symptoms	Causes
The body temperature is below 101°F (38°C) or above 103°F (38.5°C).	Various disorders
The Husky chokes and coughs	Foreign body in the throat; infection
Salivation, vomiting, perhaps diarrhea, apathy, spasms, swaying	Potential poisoning. See a veterinarian immediately.
Constipation with vomiting, lack of appetite	Potential gastric occlusion. Seek immediate emergency treatment.
The dog "scoots" on its hindquarters	Worm infestation; anal glands are obstructed
Bad mouth odor	Tooth decay, gingivitis
Repeated head shaking, head scratching	Ear inflammation
Skin disorders	Parasites, allergies, fungal infections
Attempt to vomit, bloated belly, restlessness after eating	Potential gastric torsion. Seek immediate emergency treatment.
Diarrhea, with or without blood or mucus, lack of appetite	Indigestion due to spoiled food; viral or bacterial infection; parasites; chronic enteritis
Gas, bloating, and diarrhea	Enteritis due to spoiled food
Prolapsed third eyelid; red conjunctiva; tearing, inflammation of the eyes	Possible infection
Limping, inhibition of certain movements	Tears; sprains; arthritis; hereditary problems; injuries; age-related loss of flexibility

Taking Your Dog's Temperature

Fever is characterized by an unusually warm belly and when the inner thighs feel more than warm without prior exertion of the dog. The nose is not an indicator.

Taking the body temperature is best done by two persons.

If you suspect a fever, take the dog's temperature. Get a digital thermometer with a tone signal because it works fast. Two people hold the dog; one lifts the tail and inserts the thermometer about 1½ inch (3 cm). If the temperature is above 103°F (38.5°C), the dog has a fever.

Anal and Genital Areas

If a female shows evidence of vaginal discharge without being in heat, it may be an indication of a uterine infection. Young males occasionally get an inflammation on the tip of the penis. If the anal area is caked with deposits from a bout with diarrhea, it can be easily washed off or wiped clean with a moist cloth. When your Husky "scoots" on its hindquarters it indicates that the anal glands are impacted.

First Aid for Poisoning

If you suspect that your Husky has ingested a poison, there is a window of only one-half to

Bite Wounds and Bleeding

Rough play sometimes results in bite wounds. Check your dog after such episodes. If you see a bleeding wound, cover it with a clean cloth, even if it doesn't bleed it should be treated by a veterinarian in order to prevent the formation of an abscess. Sometimes a bleeding wound is hidden by the Husky's thick coat. Part the hair gently to examine the skin more closely before you decide if the wound requires treatment.

Severely bleeding wounds from bites or other accidents need to be covered by a pressure bandage until you can get the dog to the veterinarian.

one hour in which vomiting can be induced. If you know that you cannot immediately reach a veterinarian, use a plastic syringe containing a concentrated table salt solution (1 Tbs. salt in 3½ ounces or 100 ml of water) to induce vomiting. Offer the dog lots of fresh water to drink, and follow with charcoal tablets to aid detoxification. Get veterinary help as quickly as possible!

"Scooting" on its hindquarters indicates impacted anal sacs.

How to Administer Medicine

Place pills far back on the tongue.

Pills

Hide the pill in a small piece of meat or favored snack, or open the mouth wide and place the pill at the back of the tongue, then hold the mouth closed until the dog has swallowed.

Liquid Medicine

The easiest way to administer liquid medicine is through a plastic syringe (no needle!), which you can get in pharmacies or pet stores.

Use a syringe to administer liquids.

Lift the head slightly and put the syringe through the space between the teeth from the side of the muzzle. Administer small amounts at a time to facilitate swallowing.

Suppositories

Cover the suppository with KY Jelly or with Vaseline to make it slippery; gently

Suppositories must be inserted very gently.

push it with your finger as deep into the rectum as possible, otherwise, the dog will shake it out.

Eyedrops and Ointment

Place drops inside the slightly lifted lower eyelid. Ointments may be placed either under the slightly lifted upper lid or behind the lower lid.

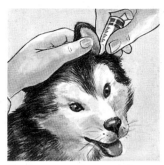

Eardrops must be carefully placed deep into the ear canal.

Eardrops

Hold the dog's head sideways so the eardrops drip deep into the ear canal. However, be careful not to put the tube into the ear.

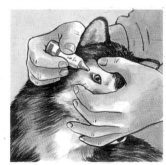

This is the proper way to administer eyedrops.

I N D E X

This posture tells you that your Husky is ready to play.

USEFUL ADDRESSES AND LITERATURE

In Europe:
Fédération Cynologique
Internationale (FCI)
13 place Albert I
B-6530 Thuin, Belgium

In the USA:
American Kennel Club (AKC)
51 Madison Avenue
New York, NY 10010
(212) 696-8200
Web Site: www.akc.org
Publisher of *The AKC Gazette*
(The most important monthly
journal for any owner of a purebred dog. In-depth articles, essential registration information,
nationwide shows and events)
Subscriptions:
(919) 233-9780
Books and videos:
(919) 233-9767

Siberian Husky Club of America,
Inc.
Corresponding secretary
Faim Zimmerman
210 Madera Drive
Victoria, TX 77905
(512) 576-5531
E-Mail: sledog@tisd.net

Breeder Contact
Carol Hines
38945 CR 653
Paw Paw, MI 49079
(616) 657-2175
E-mail: Cadobi@net-link.net

Breed Rescue
Siberian Husky Club of America
Gerry Dalakian
Flemington, NJ
(908) 782-2089
E-mail: gericksibe@aol.com

For information on breeds
that are rare, and/or not yet
recognized by the AKC:

American Rare Breed
Association
9921 Frank Tippett Road
Cheltenham, MD 20623
(301) 868-5718
Fax: (301) 868-6409
Web Site: www.arba.com
The European Kennel Reg-
istries have information on the
Internet. Starting with the Rare
Breed Association you can find all
necessary information on how to
import and register your dog, or
how to locate a breeder in the
United States, no matter how
rare the breed may be.

Dog Sledding
ISDRA (International Sled Dog
Racing Association)
(This association sanctions races,
sets rules, and safeguards safety
and fairness.)
HC 86 Box 3380
Merrifield, MN 56465
(218) 765-4297

Sled Dog Central
Everything you need to know
or buy for dog sledding.
Web Site: www.sleddogcentral.com

Alyeska Sled Dog Products
PO Box 627
Hovland, MN 55606
(218) 475-2649
www.boreal.org/alyeska

Custom Blend Foods
SDC Kushva Kennels Dog Food
St. Croix Falls, WI 54024
(715) 488-2434

Recreation for Hobby Mushers
Chugiak, Alaska
Twenty-mile kennel; personal
recreational musher facility,
20 miles outside of Anchorage.
e-mail: ourworld compuserv.
com/homepage/20 mile/

Rick Swensen's
Carlo Heights B&B
Denali, AK
1-967-683-1615

To Answer Your Questions
1. Your local pet store has
   trained staff available to
   answer your questions and to
   refer you to reading material.
2. The AKC Information Service.
3. Your local, regional, and
   national breed associations.

Liability Insurance
Most home and property insur-
ances offer liability insurance for
dogs.

Pet Health Insurance
Veterinary Pet Insurance
4175 E. La Palma Avenue,
Suite 100
Anaheim, CA 92807
(800) 872-7387

Registration
Registration is mandatory in
all cities and counties.
Call animal control offices, or
ask your local animal shelter or
your veterinarian.
If you want to prevent the
loss of your dog you should
either have your pet tattooed or
identified with a microchip. The
procedure is no more serious than
a vaccination and prevents theft
and other losses.

Further Reading
The Joy of Running Sled Dogs by
Noel Flanders (Weight pulling,
skijoring, equipment, training)
*Mush! A Beginner's Manual of
Sled Dog Training* (edited by
Bella Levorsen for Sierra
Nevada Dog Drivers)

The Author

Katharina Schlegl-Kofler has worked for many years on the subject of training dogs according to their specific breed characteristics. She specializes in the creation of puppy play school courses, and trains dogs of all kinds.

The Photographer

Ulrike Schanz took all the photographs in this book with the exception of: Wegler: cover 1. She works as a freelance photographic design artist and has specialized in animal portraiture during the past few years.

The Illustrator

Renate Holzner is a freelance artist who created the drawings in this book. Her field of expertise stretches from line drawings to photorealistic illustrations to computer graphics.

Cover Photos:

Front cover: (lg. and sm. photo) Siberian Huskies
Back cover: Husky with back packs
Page 1: Husky pulling a bike in harness for tow training
page 2/3 Huskies as cute as these wouldn't have a mischievous bone in their body, would they?
page 4/5: Playing in the snow is heavenly.
page 6/7: This Husky is expressing true happiness.
page 64: These two are preparing for trouble.

Important Information

The guidelines for the maintenance of Huskies in this book are intended for healthy, normally developed animals from high-quality breed background. If you adopt an adult Husky you must recognize that such an animal has already undergone critical imprinting by the humans with whom it has spent its formative growth phases. Even well-trained dogs can cause accidents or harm to people, and it is strongly recommended that you get liability insurance. It is also strongly recommended that you have your dog fully vaccinated and worm treated in order to prevent sickness in your pet and in its human family. Any time your Husky shows signs of illness (see page 57), you should consult a veterinarian. Some diseases are transmissible to humans (see page 54). When in doubt, consult your own physician. Some people are allergic to hair or dander. If you are not sure, consult a physician before you buy your dog.

Our Thanks

The author and publisher thank the mushers of the AGSD Training Camps Sachrang for their generous assistance, and Mr. Klaus Kennerknecht for his professional advice.

The photographer thanks the Haslbeck, Kokus, Neumayer, and Patsch families, and Mr. Srasser (Skyrunner of Universe) for allowing her to photograph their Huskies.

English translation © Copyright 1998 by Barron's Educational Series, Inc.

© 1997 by Gräfe und Unzer Verlag GmbH, München

Published originally under the title *Husky*

Consulting editor and translator: Helgard Niewisch, DVM

All inquiries should be addressed to:
Barron's Educational Series, Inc.
250 Wireless Boulevard
Hauppauge, New York 11788
http://www.barronseduc.com

Library of Congress Catalog Card No. 98-20369

International Standard Book Number 0-7641-0661-9

Library of Congress Cataloging-in-Publication Data
Schlegl-Kofler, Katharina.
    [Husky. English]
    Huskies : everything about purchase, care, nutrition, grooming, behavior, and training / Katharina Schlegl-Kofler ; photography, Ulrike Schanz ; drawings, Renate Holzner.
        p.   cm. — (A complete pet owner's manual)
        Includes bibliographical references and index.
        ISBN 0-7641-0661-9
        1. Siberian huskies. I. Title. II. Series.
SF429.S65S3413   1998
636.73—dc21
                            98-20369
                               CIP

Printed in Hong Kong
9 8 7 6 5 4 3

EXPERT ADVICE

An expert answers the most frequently asked questions on how to keep Huskies.

1 Are retractable leashes suitable for Huskies?

2 What are the reasons to neuter male Huskies?

3 What is the right age at which to spay a Husky?

4 How much will I have to spend on general supplies for sledding?

5 How should I select the various supplies?

6 Can one train an adult Husky as well as a puppy?

7 What happens at dog shows?

8 Can Huskies get overexerted?

9 What are the most fundamental important details in training Huskies?

10 What are the main purchase criteria; how much do Huskies cost?